RENEWING THE MIND OF THE MEDIA

> **"DO NOT CONFORM YOURSELVES TO THIS AGE BUT BE TRANSFORMED BY THE RENEWAL OF YOUR MIND, SO THAT YOU MAY JUDGE WHAT IS GOD'S WILL, WHAT IS GOOD, PLEASING AND PERFECT."**
>
> (ROMANS 12:2)

Statement on Overcoming the Exploitation of Sex and Violence in Communications from the U.S. Catholic Bishops

UNITED STATES CONFERENCE OF CATHOLIC BISHOPS

WASHINGTON, D.C.

Renewing the Mind of the Media was prepared by the Committee for Communications and approved by the USCC Administrative Board in March 1998 for presentation to the full membership of the United States Catholic Conference in June 1998. *Renewing the Mind of the Media* was then approved by a vote of 207-11 and is authorized for publication by the undersigned.

Monsignor Dennis M. Schnurr
General Secretary, NCCB/USCC

Unless otherwise noted, Scripture texts used in this work are taken from the *New American Bible*, copyright © 1970 by the Confraternity of Christian Doctrine, Washington, D.C. 20017 and are used by permission of copyright owner. All rights reserved.

First Printing, October 1998
Second Printing, January 2002

ISBN 1-57455-286-4

introduction

The media have such potential to bring truth and beauty into the lives of billions of people that we cannot permit them to be the arena of those who would pervert God's gifts of the body and sexuality. While today's large media conglomerates seem beyond the reach of the influence of the ordinary person, we still dare to hope, through the grace of God (whose power made the wonders of communication possible) that all those who work in or use the media will unite to magnify God's glory and to eliminate everything that would diminish his image in creation.

Because of their enormous power to shape humanity's destiny, the means of social communication are of considerable interest to the Church. As the Second Vatican Council acknowledged, the media are capable of leading the human race upward or to ruin (cf. Second Vatican Council, *The Decree on the Instruments of Social Communications* [*Inter Mirifica*], no. 11).

Contemporary means of communication have made the depiction of pornography and graphic, gratuitous violence more intense and widespread. Though not legally obscene or as offensively violent, nearly equally objectionable uses of sex and violence have become prevalent even in some forms of mainstream media. Short of these extremes, the media often use sex and violence in a frivolous and titillating way that causes a great deal of concern because it pervades the media, both news and entertainment programs. All of this has contributed to the loss of a sense of an objective right and wrong in these matters.

Pornography, excessive violence, and other irresponsible uses of sex and violence in the media gravely harm the moral and psychological health of both society as a whole and its individual members—children and adults. Even people who do not consume a great deal of media are well aware that they live in a society whose environment and values are affected by media influence for good or ill, and they can be affected themselves, even indirectly.

Today the media affect our lives more than ever. The Internet, unknown to most until quite recently, is now an essential tool for business, education, and other kinds of communication. CD-ROM technology puts at our finger-tips whole libraries and creates learning paths that enable users to grasp complex and unfamiliar subjects. Through satellite delivery and cable systems, consumers have access to many more TV channels, resulting in the availability of entertainment and information "on demand." New channels, devoted to topics such as history, government, education, science, children, foreign languages, and religion, fulfill one of television's original goals of helping to educate society, especially children, about life, culture, and the world. As the era of High Definition Television dawns, its digital technology will provide the television industry with the means of having an even larger role in the life of the home.

The media's dark side, however, continues to obscure the value of these contributions. Large corporations in the entertainment and communications industries reap substantial benefits by targeting young people, in particular, through a variety of media. They bear a responsibility for appealing to developing drives and instincts that most young people have not learned to temper with maturity.

In *The Graduate* (1967) an older woman seduces a just-out-of-college boy. Audiences may have been shocked, but not enough to keep the movie from becoming a hit.

Film and television are most frequently criticized, since, in the past, they have offered the best chance for youngsters to have unsupervised access to objectionable material. However, other forms of media, new and old, also influence young people and adults to engage in morally and socially destructive forms of behavior:

The Wild Bunch (1969) shot its way into new cinematic territory with its realistic violence.

- The utility of the Internet has already been compromised by those using it to sell sex and violence or to transmit messages of hate. This gateway to a vast world of learning and information is also a means for adults and children to access obscenity, violence, and prejudice. "Adult" and hate-provoking websites appear on the Internet, as do the equivalents of adult bookstores. Parents do not want the Internet to bring into the home these kinds of environments from which they would normally protect their children, but they can feel helpless to prevent this from happening.
- Talk radio often assaults its listeners with angry or indecent remarks.
- The music industry has deservedly come under fire for the obscene and violent messages contained in some lyrics and for the bizarre and suggestive behavior seen in various music videos. Individual music groups and songs have been accused of influencing young people to engage in destructive behavior such as drug use or even suicide.
- Brutal video games entice youngsters into equating images of violent, lawless, and sadistic worlds with what is glamorous and heroic.
- Magazines that reduce people to mere sexual objects continue to proliferate, and nothing seems beyond bounds as most portrayals of sexual behavior lose their power to shock or even embarrass. Other magazines exalt aggressive and violent activities.

Both rock lyrics and the content of video games caused concern that led to parental warning labels.

- Telephone services offer sexually stimulating talk of every kind.
- Some places of entertainment make nudity their chief attraction, even when located close to schools or family neighborhoods. They demean their employees and customers and tempt those to whom they advertise their presence to take a debased view of the human person and sexuality.
- Though a few have honorably made a policy of not doing so, many home video stores offer X-rated sections and so are major contributors to the proliferation of pornography. Most also offer a variety of action/adventure selections that have the potential of encouraging violent acting out.
- Advertising is notorious for using sex to sell products, and models, some of them young enough to be mistaken for minors, appear provocatively dressed and posed in ads in magazines and on billboards, television, and the World Wide Web.

The Church acknowledges the beauty of human sexuality and the sad fact of violence in human life. She distinguishes between the irresponsible depiction of sex and violence and their possible appropriate presentation in a moral context that may be suitable for adults, although it is not suitable for children or young people and should be kept away from them. What becomes objectionable is the use made of sex and violence, not the mere fact of their depiction.

Appearing more than two decades apart, few movies aroused more concern about inspiring youthful violence than 1971's *A Clockwork Orange* (below) and 1994's *Natural Born Killers* (left).

The pornographer and those who use graphic violence to excite the vulnerable are close kin to drug dealers who prey on people's weaknesses for their own benefit. Others who use sex and violence irresponsibly to titillate an audience also do much harm.

Government, too, bears some responsibility. Deregulation has left consumers largely without government as an ally in promoting better media in this period of vast developments in their influence.

Consumers of media also share the blame. Those who freely choose to support the industries that purvey pornography and graphic violence have a responsibility not only for themselves but for all who will be trapped in what the *Catechism of the Catholic Church* (CCC) calls "the illusion of a fantasy world" filled with sex and violence. Many more consumers fail to speak out about the lesser but still offensive examples of sexually explicit or violent material which they come across every day in mainstream media.

These are among the factors that inspire this statement. The grounds for our concern are found in a faith-filled conviction about the dignity of the body and sexuality.

pornography in the light of the theology of the body and sexuality

The Christian understanding of the body and sexuality is rooted scripturally in the creation accounts in the Book of Genesis that describe God's loving creation of the body into which he breathes a life-giving spirit (cf. Gn 2:7). The human race thus brought into existence is revealed as created by God to be both male and female (cf. Gn 1:27). The Incarnation of the Son of God reaffirms the goodness of our bodily existence, and Christ elevates the natural state of sexuality found in creation to participation in the supernatural life of grace through his institution of the Sacrament of Matrimony.

Sexual intercourse is shown to be part of the divine plan of creation, as God commands humanity to "be fruitful and multiply" (cf. Gn 1:28). The biblical text eloquently sums up the intimate sharing of life achieved in the conjugal act: "That is why a man leaves his father and mother and clings to his wife, and the two of them become one body" (Gn 2:24). In making marriage a sacrament, Christ gives even greater clarity to the purpose of sexuality. It is intended to foster a loving union between spouses and for the procreation and nurture of children.

Pornography offends against the divine plan for the body and for the intimacy of sexual union. It fixates on certain normal bodily functions in an immodest and obsessive way. It offends against chastity generically and in ways that reveal its specific evil. Following the *Catechism of the Catholic Church*, we can identify several ways in which pornography harms both those who produce it and those who use it.

By putting on display both bodily functions normally kept private and acts of sexual intimacy, which belong properly to the love of husband and

Bright hopes for the contributions of computer technology— including the Internet— have been dimmed by a proliferation of products selling sex and violence.

MATURE(17+)
ANIMATED VIOLENCE
ANIMATED BLOOD & GORE

wife, pornography violates the respect due the body and robs sexual intimacy of its intrinsic meaning and purpose. In addition, those who produce pornography, distribute it, or view it are all gravely injured by the harm done to their human dignity. Whatever rationalizations may be used, each of these, in a different way, becomes degraded into an object trapped in a system for procuring illicit pleasure and profit. All involved are drawn into "the illusion of a fantasy world" (cf. CCC, no. 2354). They are deprived of their ability to grow into the mature commitment to others whose goal, for many, is the covenant of marriage and family and, for some, the sacrifice of sexual activity "for the sake of the kingdom" (cf. Mt 19:12).

The Pontifical Council for Social Communications describes the evils of behavior or character that result from pornography, such as:

- It can have a progressively desensitizing effect, gradually rendering individuals morally numb.
- It can be addictive, causing some viewers to require progressively more perverse material to achieve the same degree of stimulation.
- It can undermine marriage and family life since it demeans their sacred value.
- In some cases, it can incite its users to commit more overtly violent crimes such as rape, child abuse, and even murder (cf. Pontifical Council for Social Communications, *Pornography and Violence in the Media: A Pastoral Response*, nos. 14-17).

Some debate whether these effects actually result from pornography. From long pastoral experience, the Church knows that many people do indeed experience a connection between pornography and tendencies toward these personal and social evils. Research today supports this pastoral experience, in particular with regard to pornography that is sexually violent. Individual studies have also observed negative consequences with regard to nonviolent pornography that is degrading in its use of women as sexual objects.

If we are fully to understand what we are dealing with in pornography, the mystery of the Fall has to be taken into account. One of its consequences is that human beings find it difficult to respond to the call that God gives them in their totality. God wants the perfection of the person. Human beings, therefore, must be open to their truest and deepest desires, which arise from God's call. This achievement of perfection involves not only the individual but is inherently social in nature. We are not created "to be alone" (Gn 2:18). We come to know one another through our bodily experiences of seeing, talking, and listening to each other. God intends the affective and aggressive drives to support each other in maturation toward strong, faithful, and self-giving love. When the affective drive turns to lust and the aggressive drive to violence, both the integrity of the person and communion between persons are lost.

Life in our modern culture makes reaching the perfection to which we are called more difficult because we are presented with so many distractions from what is central to the human good. Many of these soon reveal their tawdriness, and habits connected with them can be broken. Issues involving sexuality, which offers the prospect of the most intimate experience of the drive toward social communion, are not so easily addressed. Even within morally deformed acts, there can lurk a hint of the ability to satisfy human-

Beauty and the Beast (1991) (left) showed that G-rated movies could be extremely profitable. But did the R rating hurt or help *Pretty Woman*, the 1990 blockbuster that took an unrealistic but seemingly approving view of prostitution?

ity's powerful longing for intimacy. This is the promise with which pornography often ensnares a person. The pleasure it gives is offered as a substitute for genuine intimacy. The result of this pleasure is not intimacy but a disconnection from oneself and from others. It can even become addictive. The body and its functions, including sex, are reduced to the object of increasingly bizarre fantasies that must be taken in larger doses to reproduce the thrill of the initial involvement with pornography.

In dealing with pornography, it is important not to treat only the symptom. As an illegitimate response to legitimate desires for emotional and physical intimacy, pornography must find its remedy in a conversion to an understanding of the body and sexuality found in their intrinsic meaning as well as in revelation. This conversion culminates in an active witness to the dignity of our embodied existence. It includes sensitivity to each person's need for the bond with others that God has placed in us. Such a witness enables us to overcome the deceptions of pornography that separate us from a true appreciation for our bodies.

Since sexuality, in both its proper use and its misuse, is an element of human existence, it is always present in various art forms and the media. What is not necessarily objectionable for some, however, may be inappropriate for young people or for persons with particular sensitivities. Isolating sexuality from a moral context and using it to titillate or degrade others for one's own profit or pleasure is always wrong.

depiction of violence
in the light of the
theology of the body

Much of what has been said about pornography can be applied to graphic and excessive violence in the media. In fact, there is a class of pornography that explicitly connects sexually stimulating material with appeals to the darkly aggressive side of human nature. Rape, murder, torture, mutilation, and the gratuitous portrayal of these violent acts are among those things that deny the revealed meaning of our bodily existence and the respect due to the human body as God's creation.

Portraying this kind of violence panders to what is senselessly destructive in our natures. As with pornography, in gratuitous portrayals of violence, persons are reduced to objects for the pleasure and profit of others. Their physical integrity is shown sadistically violated, not to convey any serious message about human nature but for the visual or psychological pleasure that some take in it. Disrespect for human life is engendered when individuals or masses of people are pictured being gruesomely slaughtered to provide an audience with a thrill. Thus people are drawn once again into "the illusion of a fantasy world" in which the annoyances of daily life, great or small, can efficiently and permanently be dealt with by acts of violence.

As with sexuality, the appeal of such violence needs to be understood in the context of original sin and the change of constructive instincts into destructive pathways. The strength that enables humanity to build is akin to the aggression that tears down. Scripture provides evidence of this, but also shows that Christ is victorious over heedless human violence by refusing to allow his followers to resort to violence in his defense. He makes his peaceful acceptance of death on the cross a model for all Christians.

Senseless violence was the reason for being of horror series such as *Halloween* (above), *Friday the 13th*, and *Prom Night*.

As in the case of sexuality, it is not so much the portrayal of violence that is wrong but its misuse that makes it an end in itself and draws either no consequences or the wrong ones from it. Once again, what may not be objectionable for some may not be at all suitable for others such as children and young people.

One factor that makes this issue especially urgent today is the extreme violence of our society, particularly the degree to which many young people resort to violence.

It has been reported that a majority of more than 3,000 studies over the last forty years has found a connection between violence on the screen and in real life. The 1972 *Surgeon General's Report on TV and Behavior* cited such evidence. A decade later, the National Institute of Mental Health issued a report that concluded, "In magnitude, television violence is as strongly correlated with aggressive behavior as any other behavioral variable that has been measured." A 1992 report for the American Psychological Association confirmed this conclusion, noting that "the behavior patterns established in childhood and adolescence are the foundation for lifelong patterns manifested in adulthood" (University of Nebraska Press, *Big World, Small Screen,* 1992, p. 57).

We acknowledge that attitudes and problems in the family, at school, and within other influential social groupings undoubtedly contribute to this atmosphere of violence. Nevertheless, those who control the media still have a duty to avoid seeking better ratings or profits by irresponsibly concentrating on violence that may encourage others to use it as a solution to personal or social problems. Even those who sincerely wish to provide morally significant messages—such as the futility of violence or how it destroys those who resort to it—need to consider carefully the use of graphic violence. A good message can get lost in the visceral excitement caused by vivid depictions of violence in those who may be susceptible.

Those involved in the news media need to ask themselves whether the emphasis placed on the coverage of violent crime and the often graphic nature of this coverage is warranted. If it is not, they must take responsibility for causing undue anxiety and alarm among their consumers and for their contribution to a climate in which violence becomes commonplace.

It should be noted that, while the immorality of pornography and graphic violence can be linked through the harm each does to its producers and consumers, when it comes to judging legally what is excessive and gratuitous violence, our society lacks even the ill-defined but objective standards by which it currently judges when something is obscene.

three levels of concern

With regard to the depiction of both sex and violence in the media, it may be useful to distinguish three levels of concern.

The first level is pornography itself, which denies the dignity that God gives each human being. This kind of "entertainment" degrades those who produce it and blocks the moral and emotional development of those lured into its use. Pornography robs society of its civility and becomes a source of crime, often against the exceptionally vulnerable. Society is rightly alarmed about the danger to children both in their being exposed to pornography and in the possibility of their becoming victims of sexual or other crimes. Women, more than ever, are denouncing the pornography industry that degrades and disrespects them in particular.

At this level, we are dealing with what is usually referred to in legal terms as "obscenity" and "indecency." Obscenity and child pornography are not protected by the First Amendment and are, in fact, prohibited under federal and state laws. Indecency, too, may be regulated in some manner, at least to restrict access to minors.

Besides pornography, there is a second level of concern. This is so-called "soft core" pornography (sometimes described as "erotic" as opposed to "obscene"), which is readily available in several forms. Some R-rated movies are only marginally less offensive than X-rated films. Along with the R-rated movies shown with some regularity, cable television also offers "comedy hours" with entertainers whose monologues are liberally laced with four-letter words, sexually explicit material, and demeaning jokes about bodily functions. Some producers are challenging the broadcast television networks to go beyond their customary standards to greater sexual explicitness and toward the use of nudity and profane language.

A third level of concern is material which, while not usually identified as either "hard core" or "soft core," is disturbing because it seems to be

An immature and inappropriate view of sex pervades many magazines that emphasize looks and "feeling good" about oneself.

pervasively present, offering portrayals of sex in a frivolous and titillating manner. Even programming presented for the general viewer on broadcast television networks—often at times when children are watching—contains a good deal of material like this. Included within this last category of programming is much that is to be found on soap operas, trash talk shows, and "infotainment" programs. For the sake of ratings, even news programming is pushing the edge of the envelope of what is acceptable to the home viewer with prurient stories and sexually explicit material.

This immature and inappropriate view of sex pervades many magazines, including some aimed at teenagers or young adults in which the chief asset of any person is "looks." The advice they offer about sexual conduct focuses not on morality but how to maximize "feeling good" about oneself and minimize bad outcomes of various degrees of intimacy. Many movies advertised to attract a youthful audience contain an equally exploitative use of sex.

The way in which sex is talked about is also of concern. The freedom with which sexual matters are publicly discussed decreases the seriousness with which sexuality is treated.

The *Mighty Morphin Power Rangers* (above) and sitcoms like *Friends* helped spark a national debate about TV and values that led to the TV Parental Guidelines.

Violence too can be categorized in this way. As has been noted, there is a category in which sex and violence combine to produce a fixation on coercing persons for sex in a variety of demeaning scenarios, sometimes culminating in death. This category of violence is a form of pornography and can be dealt with by the law.

Besides this hard core "pornography of violence," there is a second category that contains various degrees of "soft core" violence. Mutilations and the gruesome depictions of violent confrontations—the sight of blood gushing from wounds or the sound of bones being crushed— constitute the "entertainment" value of "action," "slasher," "kickboxer," and similar movies. Such violence is often portrayed as sport and amusement. It is not an element of the plot or characterization but the entire purpose of the piece. Many programs of this type are available on cable television. As with the portrayal of sex, the networks are being challenged to go beyond what has been their standard toward the kind of violence often found in feature films.

The third level of concern has to do with the pervasiveness with which violence, though not so extreme as at other levels, is portrayed frivolously. It is violence at this level that often gives rise to the complaints being heard about excessive violence on the news, in cartoons designed even for very young children, and at sports events.

Violent behavior often originates in disrespectful and angry talk, and too much of the media seem not only to tolerate but to encourage hostile talk. It is one thing to identify points of disagreement and quite another to showcase the most extreme and aggressive expressions on either side of an issue. A good deal of "talk radio" and some TV talk shows seem to specialize in this kind of violence.

what should be done?

While pornography that falls within the legal definition of obscenity involves the most harmful kind of material in our three levels of concern, it is also the one area in which there is legal recourse for a solution. The courts have made it abundantly clear that obscenity and child pornography are not protected speech and laws against them can be enforced. The courts have also recognized that the standards of the local community have a part in defining obscenity.

The fundamental step, therefore, in combating the pornography industry is the enforcement of the laws that exist. Church and civic groups can provide both the encouragement and information to persuade local authorities of the gravity of these crimes in themselves and of their link to crime in general. The use of pornography is too often seen as a "victimless" crime that can be safely ignored in the face of so many other demands on the legal system. It is, in fact, one of those categories of crime that affect the overall tone of society and are the breeding ground for other types of crime.

In whatever form obscenity manifests itself, the local community has the legal right to combat it, and local authorities should enforce the law.

Education on the impact of pornography is as important as law enforcement. Too many people seem to be unaware of the extent of this industry, how profitable it is, or how demeaning is the material that is produced and distributed. The Church can provide such education through the pulpit and adult education endeavors. Groups whose purpose is to combat pornography are a resource in such education efforts.

With regard to extremely sexually explicit and graphic material that is deemed legal to produce, display, purchase, and possess, as well as both sexual and violent material described at the other levels of concern, dependence on the legal system alone is insufficient to safeguard society morally. Several audiences need to address these concerns in appropriate ways:

Sexually enticing videos can be found in most video stores. These same stores usually have "action/adventure" sections containing movies that portray high degrees of violence.

GOVERNMENT

Besides doing its duty in enforcing the obscenity and child pornography laws in a variety of media, government should reassert its regulatory role with regard to the broadcast spectrum. It is clearly established in law that the spectrum is owned by the public and is only leased to those who are licensed by the government to make use of it. Licensing renewal should cease being *pro forma* and become once again a real evaluation of whether an entity has truly been broadcasting in the public interest, as indicated by consumer comments. The waning of the regulatory function—which was

Mainstream Hollywood found drama in its evil twin, the pornography industry, with *The People vs. Larry Flynt* (right), which wrapped pornography in the sanctity of the First Amendment, and *Boogie Nights* (below), which showed porn as a world inhabited by disconnected and dysfunctional individuals.

never overly burdensome—has had an enormous impact in terms of lowering standards and opening the door to increasingly offensive material.

In addition to television and radio broadcasters, cablecasters and satellite operators, too, are regulated by the government. The public should demand regulation to the extent that it can (1) affect the concentration of control over these media, (2) disallow quick sales of media outlets that attract irresponsible owners who view them as commodities able to turn a quick profit, and (3) open these outlets to a greater variety of program sources (including religious programming). We currently advocate for such regulation, and, together with other concerned groups, will continue to do so.

Appropriate attention to the Internet and other important matters such as the TV Parental Guidelines and the "V-chip," which are intended to give parents more control over their children's viewing, should not obscure equally significant developments. The advent of High Definition Television is becoming the occasion for a digital revolution in the impact of television on our lives. At this turning point, the public must be involved with these issues or have to live with the consequences.

Government censorship across a broad range of media is not feasible under our Constitution, nor is it desirable. The Church has experienced the damage inflicted by the power of the censor, where governments, hostile to all religion or to Christianity in particular, have sought to limit the reach of the gospel message. Government's role should be to use its good offices to act as a catalyst for industry self-regulation and for consumers' expression of their rights.

Special attention should be given to the on-line problem. Now that the Supreme Court has decided that much of the information on the Internet, including the World Wide Web and proprietary commercial computer networks, is constitutionally protected, the government should direct its resources to combating the material available on these sources that remain unprotected under existing obscenity and child pornography laws. It should also seek to persuade the software industry to create the products by which consumers can block unwanted material for themselves or their families.

THE ENTERTAINMENT AND MEDIA INDUSTRIES

The entertainment and media industries deserve praise for providing many thoughtful, beautiful, or simply enjoyable works. Their creativity can reflect God's own. The potential inherent in them to add to the fund of truth and beauty in the world makes even more serious the manipulation of their gifts for immoral purposes.

The world of entertainment is a large and complex one in which there are many who know the full value of the gifts they have been given. Among them are creative and performing artists, writers and directors, songwriters and musicians, graphic artists and software technicians, producers and executives, and many others. They know their industries best and how best to turn their resources away from unworthy uses and toward the good they have to offer. We encourage such conscientious leaders, especially our fellow Catholics among them, to work within their own arts to accomplish this.

TV Y: All Children. This program is designed to be appropriate for all children. The themes and elements in this program are specifically designed for a very young audience, including children from ages 2-6.

 TV Y7: Directed to Older Children. This program is designed for children age 7 and above. Themes and elements in this program may include mild fantasy violence or comedic violence, or may frighten children under the age of 7.

 TV G: General Audience. Most parents would find this program suitable for all ages. It contains little or no violence, no strong language, and little or no sexual dialogue or situations.

 TV PG: Parental Guidance Suggested. This program may contain some material that some parents would find unsuitable for younger children. The program contains one or more of the following: moderate violence (V), some sexual situations (S), infrequent coarse language (L), or some suggestive dialogue (D).

 TV 14: Parents Strongly Cautioned. This program may contain some material that many parents would find unsuitable for children under 14 years of age. This program contains one or more of the following: intense violence (V), intense sexual situations (S), strong coarse language (L), or intensely suggestive dialogue (D).

 TV MA: Mature Audiences Only. This program is specifically designed to be viewed by adults and therefore may be unsuitable for children under 17. This program may contain one or more of the following: graphic violence (V), explicit sexual activity (S), or crude indecent language (L).

The TV Parental Guidelines resulted from widespread concern about the values that television programming was bringing into the home.

Basic morality, as well as common sense, good taste, and discretion, can go a long way toward eliminating many of the concerns expressed here.

Media business leaders deserve a special word. We ask them to re-appropriate a sense of acting in the public interest. The media today seem to define themselves almost totally in business terms. With their culture-forming impact, the media must consider whether it is acceptable to justify their choices solely on market success and profitability for stockholders, while avoiding questions about their responsibility for the moral content of their products.

We also ask advertisers and the advertising industry to consider what contribution they can make to addressing the concerns expressed in this statement. Much of the media depend on advertising revenues for their existence, and the influence of sponsors and advertisers can be crucial.

Broadcasting, in particular, not only responds to the demands of its audience but also actively creates it. Broadcast television designs much of its programming to appeal to those in the under-35 age group because they are the ones with the disposable income to buy advertisers' products. As a result, others, with little or no consumer clout of this type, may cease to watch programming which does not appeal to them and which they may find offensive. Thus broadcasters may end up serving only a small portion of the general public in whose interest they should be acting.

The development of consumer advisory labeling for many forms of entertainment, such as the Television Parental Guidelines, ought not to be seen by industry leaders as an encroachment on their right to do business as they see fit. It offers them the opportunity to renew their own sense of responsibility to their customers that is inherent in their existing standards and practices and editorial procedures.

We do not wish to single out the entertainment and media industries unduly as harmful to society. We are well aware that other industries—some of which possess a great deal of social and political support—are the source of various harmful behaviors without making a contribution to society comparable to what the media can claim. The entertainment and media industries, including television, should not be scapegoated entirely for all social ills. While their influence is undeniable, it is not clear that they are the strongest such influence.

Nor do the media, again television in particular, offer only negative messages. For example, while the sexual innuendo found on most comedy programs shows a considerable moral and creative failure on the part of television, many television dramas today are superior in content to the "Dallas-Dynasty" kind of "nighttime soaps" popular in the last decade, although throwbacks can be found on the newer networks.

We also want to say a special word to the creative community. The members of this community are usually the ones most concerned that the right to self-expression not be infringed. We share your concern, for the Church too has seen her own rights infringed not only by governments hostile to religion but even by media organizations that have acted like censors. In some instances, media outlets have decided that the Church's message is "inappropriate" for their consumers or have appealed to "the separation of church and state" as an excuse for silencing values-oriented messages.

However, like many parents and religious leaders, prominent creative people have indicated reservations about the suitability for their own families of a good deal of what they see and hear today, even among their own creations. They are also concerned about the lack of messages that uplift the human spirit in so much that is produced and by the impact that the concentration on the "bottom line" has on their creative aspirations. These concerns offer points of contact for a dialogue between the creative community and the Church which has always taken seriously the influence of the arts.

The media need to consider these issues carefully. Sound ethics, professional responsibility, and good public relations would all be well served by self-regulatory mechanisms within the media industries to avoid the least common denominator of morals and taste becoming the industry standard.

THE GENERAL PUBLIC

In our consumer-oriented society, praise and blame belong not only to the media industries but also to their customers. While the media do more to shape their audiences than they admit, there are still large enough audiences seeking objectionable material to make it profitable to produce and distribute it.

If the media's choices need to be scrutinized, so do those of consumers. Some may contradict themselves by watching, listening to, or reading what they say they deplore. News coverage of sensational crimes offers proof of this phenomenon. While the public may say that such coverage is excessive, the media that cut back on it sometimes suffer an audience loss compared to the media that continue with wall-to-wall coverage.

While it is too facile for media leaders to advise consumers who do not like something to turn to another channel or other media outlet, nothing will change if consumers do not make these choices. Media are supported by those who purchase their products or those of their advertisers. If media business people make unacknowledged moral decisions by what they produce, consumers do so by what they choose to consume.

With the media so influential in shaping the way our society views the important issues of the day, it is irresponsible to be indifferent to their impact. Even those who are not naturally media-oriented have a responsibility to know enough about them to react intelligently to the media's influence.

One group of consumers especially needs to be addressed: those addicted to pornography, other sexually explicit material, and gratuitously violent material. Such people are exploited for profit by a callous underworld of the media industries. Surely these consumers themselves sense

- The time and money wasted in pursuit of the thrill that comes from this material
- Their own victimization as they come to crave ever more explicit material
- The victimization of those being exploited for their pleasure
- The victimization of society faced with the loss of the beneficial contributions that could have been made by those who become fixated on this material or the prospect of criminal behavior on the part of those who use and produce it

We call on these consumers to get the help they need, and we urge our parishes, through educational efforts, preaching, counseling, and the celebration of the Sacrament of Reconciliation, to provide help.

PARENTS AND YOUNG PEOPLE

On several occasions, the Lord expressed his compassion for those whom he saw burdened with life's troubles. We are reminded of his compassion when we hear from parents about all the difficulties they must overcome in raising their children in an environment not always conducive to their healthy development. Parents are often frustrated by the influence of other forces seemingly beyond their control, including the media.

We urge them not to be too quick to denigrate their own influence. There is a bond between parents and children that nothing else can replace no matter how much, at any given moment, children seem to look elsewhere for example and guidance. The influences that parents fear have the most room to flourish where they do not offer their own moral direction. Families should use the media together instead of, as is common today, in isolated units. Used properly, the media can provide both learning and pleasure.

While we hesitate to place additional burdens on parents in today's complex world, we urge them, as a priority, to know the media to which their children relate and to help them understand the messages they send. Parents should be clear about the media they reject. Sharing the reasons why a video game is too

NYPD Blue's debut got hit with calls for boycotts for its experiments with partial nudity and profane language on broadcast television.

violent or a particular TV show lacks good values about sex can contribute to a youngster's moral growth. Parents should also encourage a sense of discipline when it comes to the media. There must be time when the almost continuous noise from televisions, radios, computers, and telephones—often even while the family is together for meals —gives way to quieter times for family discussion, prayer, and homework. Many parents, no less than children, need to become less media dependent.

Included in this media discipline is the proper use of the Internet and other on-line services that can be of great benefit but also an excuse to waste time and an occasion for bringing into the home gravely objectionable material.

In all media, parents should be aware of the availability to and use by their children of material that is the beginning of an attraction to what is pornographic and excessively violent. Parents' own example in rejecting such material as unworthy of attention is crucial.

Teenage men, even some who are active in the Church, are among the most susceptible to the influence of pornography. The temptation to use things like sexually explicit videos or phone-sex lines can make it easy to rationalize their effect. However, using them enables pornography to be present in the heart of society and not only at its margins. The same can be said of graphically violent material.

In these matters, as in so many others, we ask our young people to live up to the idealism that has been characteristic of them and a regular resource for good. Parents ought to encourage their children to play an active role in developing the cures for the ills under discussion. In opposing pornography and excessive violence in the media, young people have the outlet for a fresh and enthusiastic witness to their convictions about the respect that is every person's due. The entertainment and media industries have such an intense focus on youth that media-literate young people are in a position to make a significant impact on them.

We encourage our Catholic youth to speak out against the abusive manipulation they are subjected to by media. Families and young people, especially working together in church and community groups, are an indispensable force for limiting the influence of those who would misuse the power of communication and for encouraging those who use it well.

CHURCH LEADERS

The last audience we wish to address is church leaders, ourselves included. We must give witness to the truth about the body and sexuality of which we have spoken. Our own example of chastity and a peaceful spirit will

The Film and Broadcasting Office of the United States Conference of Catholic Bishops reviews and rates more than 250 movies a year as well as hundreds of home video releases and significant television shows.

make us effective witnesses to the worth and dignity of every person, the beauty of sexuality used within God's plan for it, and the inappropriateness of violence as a solution to personal and social problems.

As educators, we are obliged to help our people identify and articulate these issues. As preachers, we should call them to turn away from an indifference which allows the media to diminish respect for the human person. As leaders, we must bring our people together on these issues and organize them to exert the influence that we, as Church, can have. As healers, we need to offer the appropriate help to all wounded by the misuse of sex and violence in the media, above all through the Sacrament of Reconciliation. Lastly, we need humbly to ask our people's support, so that when we speak as moral leaders, our voices will be heeded by those we hope to influence.

appendix 1
seven practical steps

1. **FOR DIOCESES:** Establish a task force, possibly with the diocesan communications office as lead agent, to develop educational programs on the problem of pornography and—perhaps with ecumenical and interfaith participation—to determine the extent of the problem of the distribution of obscene or indecent material and entertainment in your area. Share the results with local law enforcement officials and demand action. Work with the chamber of commerce to create an environment which allows no room in the community for entertainment that exploits sex and violence.

2. **FOR PARISHES:** Develop media discussion groups to enable parents to talk about what is on television or in other media, and to encourage mutual learning and support in guiding their children's media choices. The problems of pornography and graphic violence should be included in homilies on appropriate occasions.

3. **FOR FAMILIES:** Arrange for a monthly or weekly media-free day, at home or away from home, so that communication will be mostly among family members. Use this time to talk about the problems addressed in this statement as well as other ways in which the media affect family life, for example, through advertising.

4. **FOR CATHOLIC EDUCATORS:** Develop media discussion groups for teachers and students. Regularly identify everyone's three or four favorite television programs, songs, music videos, magazines, and on-line activities. View or listen to some of these together and discuss what moral messages come through.

5. **FOR THE MEDIA CREATIVE AND BUSINESS COMMUNITIES:** Set up dialogues with other interested people, especially parents, to discuss the impact your media productions are having.

6. **FOR GOVERNMENT:** Reassert regulatory functions that take into account public interest obligations of various media.

7. **FOR EVERYONE:** Develop a list of addresses, phone/fax numbers, and e-mail addresses of local media outlets. Ask yourself what media portrayal of sex or violence has most offended you recently, and then contact the media outlet responsible to complain. Alternatively, ask yourself what is the best thing you've seen in the media recently and contact that media outlet with your thanks. Make this a habit. Join media action groups set up by your parish, diocese, or interdenominationally.

appendix 2
framework for dealing with legislation and court cases involving obscenity and indecency or excessive violence

1. With regard to legislation and court cases involving obscenity or indecency and, potentially, excessive and graphic violence, the United States Conference of Catholic Bishops is concerned about the impact of this material on society, both on adults and especially on young people, who inevitably lack the perspective to deal with such material in a mature and morally responsible fashion.

2. Parents have the primary responsibility to protect their children from objectionable material. Children and young people need not only protection but also positive education in authentic values by parents and other significant adults. Without considering them solutions, the Conference supports the "V" chip and the TV Parental Guidelines as steps to assist parents.

3. The constitutional right to free speech is basic to our democratic society. This right does not and ought not extend to the socially and morally detrimental speech that is obscenity. To those who exercise the right of free speech belongs the responsibility of resisting demands for other forms of harmful speech such as indecency and excessive and graphic violence. Government does not violate the freedom of speech when it

encourages measures for self-regulation by the entertainment and media industries. Such self-regulation is not only appropriate but also an obligation, given the seriousness with which the public views the media's often negative impact.

4. The problem of objectionable material is only partially solved by current laws on obscenity and indecency that do not deal with excessive and graphic violence. There is room for revision in the laws, regulations, and court decisions that govern these matters. A nuanced definition of excessive violence is needed to aid both legislators and self-regulators. While in a pluralistic society it may be necessary to live with results that fall short of the optimum, groups within society can do much to help their members, as exemplified by the work of the USCC Office of Film and Broadcasting with its reviews and ratings of films, most of which have been gathered into the *Guide for Family Viewing* and its reviews of television programming.

5. We do not support government restrictions on gathering and reporting news. To avoid the presentation of material that might be harmful to children and young people, news organizations should be urged to set up a uniform code of standards and practices and monitor compliance with it.

6. The Internet, including the World Wide Web and proprietary commercial computer networks, raise new challenges. They have the potential to bring into the home material harmful to children and young people at a time when they often have more computer skills than their parents. Since the Supreme Court has extended First Amendment protections to computer speech, the laws applicable to unprotected speech, such as child pornography, must be enforced in on-line circumstances. The on-line industry should work with parents to develop mechanisms to protect children effectively. Young people's access to computers outside the home needs to be dealt with both by self-regulation on the part of those involved and constitutionally sound legislation.

appendix 3
american media profile

U.S. households:	99.6 million

RADIO

Households with radios:	98.6 million
Radio advertising revenue:	$12.4 billion

TV

Households with TV sets:	98 million
TV sets per household:	2.3
Average viewing time per day:	7 hours, 15 minutes
. . . for teenage viewers:	3 hours, 2 minutes
. . . for children viewers:	3 hours, 7 minutes
TV advertising revenue:	$28.4 billion
Cable subscribers:	64.8 million
Direct satellite subscribers:	10.2 million
Cable fees and advertising revenue:	$23 billion

VIDEOS

Households with VCRs:	85.26 million
Number of video stores:	28,000
Average video rental price:	$2.75
Home video revenues:	$15 billion

MOVIES

Movie box-office gross:	$6.2 billion
Weekly admissions:	25.7 million
Percentage of admissions by age:	
12-39 years old:	67%
40 years old and over:	32%
Average admission price:	$4.42
Total movie screens:	29,731

COMPUTERS

Households with computers:	36.4 million
Households with e-mail:	16.8 million
Households with access to on-line services:	18.5 million

MEDIA INDUSTRY

Recording industry revenues:[1]	$12.2 billion
Cassette sales:	$2.2 billion
CD sales:	$8.5 billion
Daily newspapers:	1,509
Magazines published:[2]	18,047
U.S. book sales:	$21.3 billion

Sources: *1998 International Television and Video Almanac;* the National Association of Theatre Owners; *Editor and Publisher;* U.S. Department of Commerce/National Telecommunications and Information Administration, *Falling Through the Net II: New Data on the Digital Divide,* July 28, 1998; Recording Industry Association of America, *1997 Consumer Profile;* Association of American Publishers

NOTES

1 Includes all categories: CDs, cassettes, music videos, etc.

2 Includes all frequencies: weekly, biweekly, monthly, etc.

appendix 4
network and cable tv
addresses

Consumers can contact the following network and cable companies to express their concerns about the depiction of pornography and graphic, gratuitous violence.

ABC: 77 West 66th St., New York, NY 10023

A&E Network or The History Channel: 235 East 45th St.,
New York, NY 10017

American Movie Classics (AMC) or Bravo: 150 Crossways Park West,
Woodbury, NY 11797

Black Entertainment Television (BET): 1900 W. Pl., NE,
Washington, DC 20018

Cable News Network (CNN), Cartoon Network, CNN Headline News,
TBS SuperStation, Turner Classic Movies, or Turner Network
Television: One CNN Center, P.O. Box 105366, Atlanta, GA 30348

CBS: 51 West 52nd St., New York, NY 10019

Cinemax or HBO: 1100 Ave. of the Americas, New York, NY 10036

CNBC or MSNBC: 2200 Fletcher Ave., Fort Lee, NJ 07024

Comedy Central: 1775 Broadway, New York, NY 10019

Court TV: 600 Third Ave., Second Floor, New York, NY 10016

C-SPAN: 400 North Capitol St., NW, Suite 650, Washington, DC 20001

The Discovery Channel or The Learning Channel: 7700 Wisconsin Ave., Bethesda, MD 20814-3522

The Disney Channel: 3800 West Alameda Ave., Burbank, CA 91505

E! Entertainment Television: 5670 Wilshire Blvd., Los Angeles, CA 90036

Encore or Starz!: 5445 DTC Pkwy., Suite 600, Englewood, CO 80111

ESPN: ESPN Plaza, 935 Middle St., Bristol, CT 06010

The Family Channel: 2877 Guardian Ln., P.O. Box 2050, Virginia Beach, VA 23450-2050

Flix, Showtime, or The Movie Channel: 1633 Broadway, New York, NY 10019

Fox Broadcasting Company: P.O. Box 900, Beverly Hills, CA 90213

Fox News Channel: 1211 Ave. of the Americas, New York, NY 10036

fX or fXM: Movies from Fox: P.O. Box 900, Beverly Hills, CA 90213-0900

Galavision or Univision: 9405 NW 41 St., Miami, FL 33178

Lifetime: 309 West 49th St., New York, NY 10019

MTV, Nickelodeon, or VH1: 1515 Broadway, New York, NY 10036

The Nashville Network: 2806 Opryland Dr., Nashville, TN 37214

NBC: 30 Rockefeller Plaza, New York, NY 10112

PBS: 1320 Braddock Pl., Alexandria, VA 22314-1698

Sci Fi Channel or USA Network: 1230 Ave. of the Americas, New York, NY 10020

Telemundo: 2290 West Eighth Ave., Hialeah, FL 33010

United Paramount Network (UPN): P.O. Box 251735, Los Angeles, CA 90025

WB Television Network: 4000 Warner Blvd., Building 34 R, Burbank, CA 91522

WGN: 2501 W. Bradley Pl., Chicago, IL 60618